Editor
Kim Fields

Managing Editor
Mara Ellen Guckian

Illustrator
Kelly McMahon

Cover Artists
Kevin Barnes
Barb Lorseyedi

Editor in Chief
Ina Massler Levin, M.A.

Creative Director
Karen J. Goldfluss, M.S. Ed.

Art Coordinator
Renée Christine Yates

Imaging
James Edward Grace
Craig Gunnell

Publisher

Mary D. Smith, M.S. Ed.

Rhymes, Riddles & to Make Kids Think

Grade Pre-K

Quick & easy activities to develop

- creative-thinking skills
- problem-solving skills
- visual discrimination

Author

Lynne R. Weaver, M.S.

Teacher Created Resources, Inc.
6421 Industry Way
Westminster, CA 92683
www.teachercreated.com

ISBN: 978-1-4206-2559-2

© 2009 Teacher Created Resources, Inc.
Made in U.S.A.

Teacher Created Resources

Table of Contents

Introduction

Young learners need to learn confidence and creativity. The development of creative thinking skills is essential to participate in today's changing world. The activities included in *Rhymes, Riddles, and Reasoning Activities (Preschool)* encourage children to develop thinking skills in fun and creative ways. These engaging exercises will contribute to a child's natural desire to receive information and apply it to new and challenging situations.

Preschool teachers *and* parents will enjoy using this book. The suggested activities provide opportunities for children to look at a topic, problem, or situation from several different perspectives; develop questions; challenge preconceived notions; take risks; brainstorm; and apply previously acquired information. Using all of these tools, the children will look at problems or tasks in new ways to arrive at creative solutions.

The ideas presented in this book address the many facets of early childhood education. Since preschool students love to move around, activities have been included to encourage active participation. Children also love to play with language. How often do you hear a group of students repeating the same chant? This is because of their love for the rhythm of language. The many rhyming activities in *Rhymes, Riddles, and Reasoning Activities (Preschool)* address this stage of a child's development. Children can gain a deeper understanding of math concepts while they are participating in the math-related activities. Finally, basic problem-solving activities are included, covering a wide range of topics.

Children practice listening and taking turns, developing creative-thinking skills, speaking in complete sentences, talking in front of their peers, and having fun. Teachers benefit too. They can closely observe each child as he or she performs a task and offer valuable compliments to help build a child's confidence. In addition, by focusing on one child at a time, the remaining children have the opportunity to hear the responses of their peers and learn from them.

The activities suggested in this book are easy to implement during group time (circle) in approximately 10 to 15 minutes. Many of the activities offer a suggested list of questions. Some make use of common classroom materials, and others require items that are readily available.

Remember that each class has children with varying abilities. It is imperative to have a basic grasp of each child's ability and tailor the questions accordingly. Choose a child who has a good understanding of the skill to begin with, and let the other children watch and learn as the activity proceeds. Occasionally, a child will hesitate to answer. This is a good time to say something such as "I like the way Isaac is thinking about his answer." This takes some of the pressure off the child and rewards him or her for not rushing and guessing. Then, if necessary, guide the child to a successful outcome. As children respond, the teacher needs to acknowledge their answers in a positive manner. If a child's response is incorrect, then the teacher can assist the child to find the correct answer.

Each time a new type of activity is introduced, the teacher needs to model how to answer the question or perform the required task. The very nature of these activities will help develop the child's ability to express himself or herself.

Get started and have fun! The learning will come naturally.

Getting Started

Have children sit together in a close, intimate group such as circle or whole group time. (It will usually take 10 to 15 minutes to complete an activity included in this book once students are familiar with the process. This is just the right amount of time for a group activity!) It is important for all children to be able to see the visual aids used and hear the responses from their classmates. Explain that you will describe the activity and then give a demonstration. For example, you might ask, "What is your favorite toy?" Model the correct way to answer the question by saying, "My favorite toy is my doll." Try to use complete sentences for all responses.

The following examples provide good topics for a new group of students: What is your favorite food? Do you have any brothers or sisters? What is your favorite story or book? Ask each child the same question. Follow each response with a positive comment, so that each child will feel validated and enjoy the activity. When you get off to a good start, the children look forward to this part of each day's routine. Keep in mind that there might be several correct answers.

How to Use This Book

The teacher should preview the material before using it. If the class has less than 20 students, the teacher can choose the questions that would be most appropriate for individual students. Likewise, if the class is larger, the teacher can add additional questions before presenting the activity.

Occasionally, there is more than one correct answer to a question. The children can use the information they have learned to make choices, examine relationships, and explore new possibilities. It is fun for children to realize that there are many correct answers. All of this leads to a deeper understanding and appreciation that there is more than one way to arrive at a solution. Have fun stimulating young thinkers with a variety of activities.

The activities in this book are organized alphabetically to make it easier to find a topic. Many of the activities described will use classroom supplies. A list of supplies needed and the directions for each activity are provided. Some of the materials the teacher will use include classroom manipulatives, a bulletin board, a chalkboard, and the children themselves. In addition, some activities will use materials described in this book and/or provided patterns to make specific materials.

Storage

Use a notebook or file folder to store the visual aids after making them. This book and the teacher-created file will provide a valuable resource that the teacher can use throughout the school year.

Act It Out

Materials

- Act It Out Cards (this page and pages 6–8)
- construction paper
- markers
- scissors
- glue sticks

Directions for the Teacher

1. Make copies of the Act It Out Cards on this page and pages 6–8.
2. Color, cut out, and mount the cards onto construction paper. Laminate the cards.
3. Place the cards face down in a pile.

Procedure

1. Ask children to think about acting for this activity.
2. Each child will pick one Act It Out Card. The child will then act as the card indicates without using any props.
3. The other children will guess what he or she is doing.

Possible Actions

- Blowing a bubble
- Blowing nose
- Brushing long hair
- Brushing teeth
- Buttoning a shirt
- Cutting toenails
- Doing pushups
- Eating a big sandwich
- Eating an ice-cream cone
- Fishing—pulling in a big fish
- Flying a kite
- Giving an adult a hug
- Hammering a nail
- Painting a picture
- Playing basketball
- Pulling a wagon
- Pushing a heavy bookcase
- Putting on shoes
- Sleeping
- Throwing a ball

Act It Out Cards

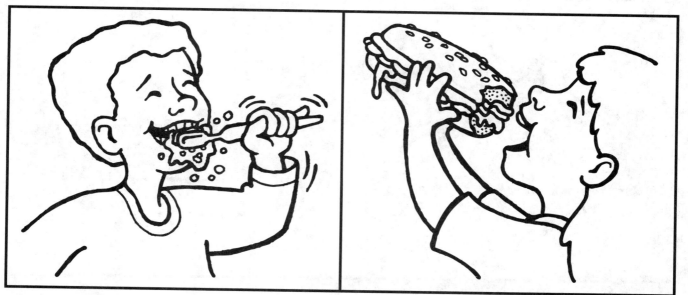

Act It Out Cards *(cont.)*

6

Act It Out Cards *(cont.)*

Act It Out Cards *(cont.)*

8

After the Storm

Materials

- After the Storm Story (page 10)
- After the Storm Patterns (pages 10–11)
- tagboard
- 20 craft sticks
- markers
- permanent marker
- small tabletop or floor area (to display activity)

Directions for the Teacher

1. Make copies of the After the Storm Patterns on pages 10–11. Color the patterns, cut them out, and mount them onto tagboard. Cut out the patterns and laminate.

2. Cut a small slit in each pattern where indicated. Attach the stands to the patterns. (See diagram above.)

3. On each craft stick, write a number from 1–20 on both sides. (These will be the wooden posts used to mark the trail.)

4. Set up the house and cabin, placing the trail posts between them. It should be displayed so that the children are looking at the trail posts from left to right. (See illustration below.)

Procedure

1. Read or tell the story (see page 10) about the scientist, Mr. Roberts.

2. After reading the story, ask the children to help rearrange the wooden posts so Mr. Roberts can find his way home.

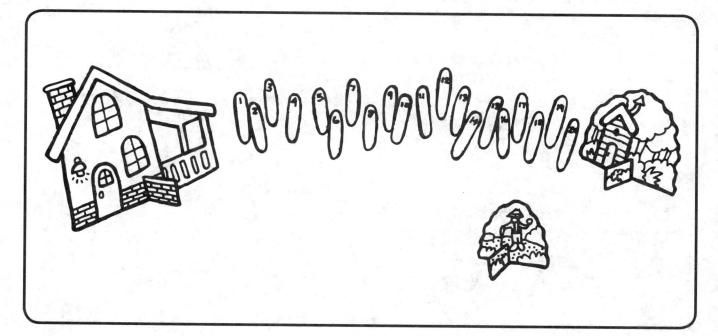

After the Storm *(cont.)*

Story

A scientist named Mr. Roberts lived on a huge farm in the country. On the edge of his farm there was a wonderful forest where he would go to learn about the plants and animals that lived in the forest. He loved to spend hours observing the animals and exploring. Mr. Roberts painted numbers on wooden posts leading the way into the woods so he could spend time exploring without worrying about getting lost. At the end of the trail was his special little cabin where he would write notes and keep his wonderful collections.

One day, Mr. Roberts decided to go to the woods for an afternoon of discovery. He carefully followed the wooden posts as they marked the trail. *(Move Mr. Roberts slowly past the post signs, counting each one as you pass it. At the same time, interject the next sentence.)* As he was hiking into the woods, Mr. Roberts saw a mother deer and her baby fawn, he passed some beautiful flowers just ready to open, and he crossed under an old bridge where he saw hundreds of tadpoles swimming in the cool water.

Mr. Roberts spent most of the morning exploring and following his special trail. Suddenly, it started to rain. Mr. Roberts did not want to walk home in the rain, so he decided to stay in the cabin until the rain stopped. Then it got very dark. The rain started pouring, and the wind whipped through the trees. *(Mix up all the numbered posts.)* He was glad he had decided not to walk home. The storm quickly passed, and he was ready to go back to his big house on the farm for dinner. As he turned onto the trail, he noticed that the last trail post was missing. In fact, all the trail posts were missing. The wind had knocked them down and scattered them throughout the woods!

Discussion

"How is Mr. Roberts going to get home? Do you think we could help him find his way home? Let's work together to help. The last number on his trail posts was number 20. We will need to count down (backward) to help Mr. Roberts find his way home. Who can help me find the number 20?" Call on different children until each number is in the correct spot. Be sure to thank the children for helping Mr. Roberts find his way home.

After telling this story to the class, leave the "wooden posts" out for the children to arrange in the correct order during free time.

After the Storm Patterns

After the Storm Patterns *(cont.)*

Alphabet Erase

Materials
- chalkboard or whiteboard
- appropriate writing tool
- small eraser for board

Procedure
1. Ask the children to help say the alphabet as the teacher writes it on the board. (Write the letters in alphabetical order for younger children. Mix up the order for older children.)
2. Read the introduction to the class.
3. Read one line from the poem for each child.
4. Allow the child to erase the letter from the board.

Introduction
The alphabet is fun to say, but some of the letters will not stay.
Listen carefully as I read each clue, when it is your turn, you will know what to do.

Poem

We use letters to learn to spell; please erase the letter **L**.

It is not hard to see; please erase the letter **Z**.

I do not want to cry; please erase the letter **I**.

It will not be hard to see; please erase the letter **G**.

It will be a help to me; if you can, erase the letter **B**.

I just want to say; please erase the letter **A**.

I think you can do this for me; please erase the letter **D**.

I think we will all feel free; if you erase the letter **E**.

We must not move too slow; please erase the letter **O**.

The alphabet starts with the letter **A**; please erase the letter **J**.

Isn't this a funny day; please erase the letter **K**.

This letter is a gem; please erase the letter **M**.

I have a friend named Ben; please erase the letter **N**.

This is fun, golly gee; please erase the letter **P**.

This will not be hard for you; please erase the letter **Q**.

You will not have to look far; please erase the letter **R**.

You will not need to guess; please erase the letter **S**.

The letters are disappearing you see; please erase the letter **T**.

This is a special request for you; please erase the letter **U**.

I am sure that you will see; please erase the letter **V**.

I have a dog, his name is Rex; please erase the letter **X**.

Make sure you use your eye; please erase the letter **Y**.

There will not be many letters left; if you can, erase the letter **F**.

Note: The letters **C, H,** and **W** are not included in the poem. When everyone in the class has had a turn to erase one letter, ask the group to identify the letters remaining on the board.

12

Around the House

Materials

- Around the House Cards (pages 14–18)
- construction paper
- markers

Directions for the Teacher

1. Make copies of the Around the House Cards on pages 14–18.
2. Color, cut out, and mount the cards onto construction paper. Laminate the cards.

Procedure

1. Set up the Around the House Cards so the children can easily see them.
2. Read one riddle to each child. (Remind children to listen to all the clues before answering.)
3. Have the child find the card that the riddle describes.

Around the House Riddles

1. You add soap and turn me on. I get your clothes clean. What am I? **WASHING MACHINE**

2. You use me to get a good night's sleep. I have a pillow and blankets. What am I? **BED**

3. You dial a number to talk to people. When someone wants to talk to you, I ring. What am I? **TELEPHONE**

4. You turn me on, and I make lots of noise. I cut grass. What am I? **LAWN MOWER**

5. You use me to keep your food cold and fresh. I have a door. What am I? **REFRIGERATOR**

6. You plug me in, and I help clean the carpet and rugs. What am I? **VACUUM CLEANER**

7. You turn me on so you can watch a show or the news. What am I? **TV**

8. You can use me to learn new things. Turn on my screen and use the keyboard. What am I? **COMPUTER**

9. Adults use me to get wrinkles out of clothes. I am hot when plugged in! What am I? **IRON**

10. You can use me to take pictures when you are having a special celebration. What am I? **CAMERA**

11. You use me to get the dishes clean. Add soap and turn me on. What am I? **DISHWASHER**

12. You sit in me to clean your body. Add a washcloth and soap. What am I? **BATHTUB**

13. You ride in me. I have four wheels, a horn, a trunk, and doors. What am I? **CAR**

14. You use me to ride from one place to another. I have wheels. I might have a bell. What am I? **BICYCLE**

15. You use me to see in your house at night. Turn me on with a switch. What am I? **LAMP**

16. You use me to bake a cake or make a pizza. Make sure to use potholders. What am I? **OVEN**

17. You use me to protect your car. I also hold bikes, lawn mowers, and ladders. What am I? **GARAGE**

18. You use me to store your clothes. I keep them organized. I have drawers. What am I? **DRESSER**

19. You use me to listen to music. I have buttons and knobs. What am I? **RADIO/MP3 PLAYER**

20. You sit at me for a meal. I can be in the kitchen or dining room. What am I? **TABLE**

Around the House Cards

Around the House Cards *(cont.)*

Around the House Cards *(cont.)*

Around the House Cards (cont.)

Around the House Cards *(cont.)*

18

Attributes

Materials
- Attribute Cards (pages 20–25)
- construction paper
- markers

Directions for the Teacher
1. Make copies of the Attribute Cards on pages 20–25. Color the cards, cut them out, and mount them onto construction paper.
2. Make copies of the boxes below and cut them out. Glue each box, listing possible attributes, onto the back of the corresponding card.
3. Laminate the cards for durability.

Procedure
1. Display one card so all the children can see it.
2. Make up a sentence using one of the attributes suggested on the back of the card.
3. Ask a child to identify the correct object. For example, "Jamal, can you point to the animal in the middle?" "Rosita, can you point to the longest snake?"
4. Use each card to have the children identify several different attributes.

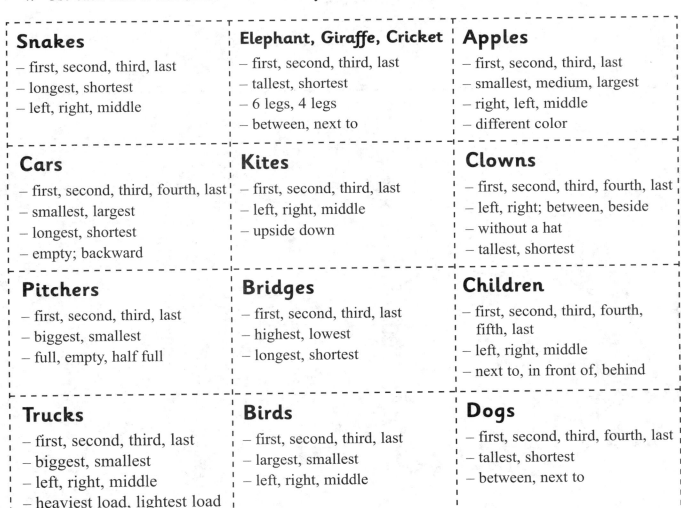

Snakes
- first, second, third, last
- longest, shortest
- left, right, middle

Elephant, Giraffe, Cricket
- first, second, third, last
- tallest, shortest
- 6 legs, 4 legs
- between, next to

Apples
- first, second, third, last
- smallest, medium, largest
- right, left, middle
- different color

Cars
- first, second, third, fourth, last
- smallest, largest
- longest, shortest
- empty; backward

Kites
- first, second, third, last
- left, right, middle
- upside down

Clowns
- first, second, third, fourth, last
- left, right; between, beside
- without a hat
- tallest, shortest

Pitchers
- first, second, third, last
- biggest, smallest
- full, empty, half full

Bridges
- first, second, third, last
- highest, lowest
- longest, shortest

Children
- first, second, third, fourth, fifth, last
- left, right, middle
- next to, in front of, behind

Trucks
- first, second, third, last
- biggest, smallest
- left, right, middle
- heaviest load, lightest load

Birds
- first, second, third, last
- largest, smallest
- left, right, middle

Dogs
- first, second, third, fourth, last
- tallest, shortest
- between, next to

Attribute Cards

Attribute Cards *(cont.)*

Attribute Cards *(cont.)*

Attribute Cards (cont.)

Attribute Cards *(cont.)*

Attribute Cards *(cont.)*

Community Helpers

Procedure

1. Review with the children that people have many different kinds of jobs in their community. Each person's job is important and will help the children feel safe and secure in their town.

2. Explain to the children that you are going to describe a community helper, and they will tell who has the special job that you are describing.

3. Explain to the class that there may be several correct answers. (Occasionally, the children may answer that their parents do a particular job. This is a good time to introduce the new vocabulary of various community helpers.)

4. Encourage the children to answer in complete sentences.

Community Helpers

Who can help when . . .

1. my house is on fire? **FIREFIGHTER**

2. I want to get my hair cut in a new style? **HAIRDRESSER/HAIR STYLIST**

3. my sister has an ear infection? **DOCTOR**

4. my mom wants fresh corn for dinner? **FARMER /GROCERY WORKER**

5. my big brother needs to write a report about rocket ships? **LIBRARIAN**

6. I want to learn how to swim? **SWIMMING COACH/TEACHER**

7. I want to mail a package to my grandfather? **POSTAL WORKER**

8. I need to get all the garbage out of my house and into the landfill? **GARBAGE COLLECTOR**

9. I want to make sure my teeth are healthy and strong? **DENTIST**

10. I spill juice at school? **TEACHER/CLASSMATE**

11. my brother wants to learn how to play soccer? **COACH**

12. I want to buy some flowers for my mom's birthday? **FLORIST**

13. my father falls off a ladder and breaks his leg? **AMBULANCE DRIVER/EMT**

14. I want to get a special cake for my grandma's birthday? **BAKERY WORKER/BAKER**

15. my cat is sick and I am worried about her? **VETERINARIAN**

16. I need to fly on a plane to another city to visit my cousins? **PILOT/FLIGHT ATTENDANT**

17. I want to eat in a fancy restaurant and order from a menu? **WAITER/WAITRESS**

18. my brother wants to learn how to do magic tricks? **MAGICIAN/LIBRARIAN**

19. my big sister wants to learn about the animals at the zoo? **ZOOKEEPER/ZOO VOLUNTEER**

20. my father wants to build a new house? **CARPENTER/HOME BUILDER**

Find the Mistakes

Materials
- Find the Mistakes cards (pages 28–32)
- Answer Key Cards (below)
- markers
- construction paper

Directions for the Teacher
1. Make copies of the Find the Mistakes cards on pages 28–32. Color the cards, cut them out, and mount them onto construction paper.
2. Copy and cut out the Answer Key Cards (below). Glue them onto the back of the appropriate cards. Then laminate the cards.

Procedure
1. Use one card at a time. Place it so the children can easily see the picture. Ask a child to find and describe a mistake on the card. (Use each card with four or five students before moving to a new card. This ensures that each child will have more than one opportunity to find something wrong.)
2. Call on one child at a time until everyone has had a chance to participate.
3. Repeat each child's sentence. If necessary, expand on the sentence using the proper vocabulary and sentence structure. Example: "That's right, the dog is reading a newspaper, and we know that dogs don't read!"

Answer Key Cards

Page 28—Farm Scene
- duck wearing boots
- horse has a pig tail
- farmer wearing scuba gear
- dog driving a tractor
- cat dressed in tutu, standing on hind legs
- fish swimming above the pond

Page 29—City Scene
- police officer directing traffic, sitting on a turtle
- street vendor wearing bathing suit when everyone else is wearing winter coats
- words on the bus are upside down
- dog reading a newspaper, wearing clothes and standing on 2 legs
- car has square wheels
- street vendor's cart umbrella is upside down
- doors on building are different styles

Page 30—Zoo Scene
- bear, holding a balloon, is outside of cage
- penguin, leaning against a cactus, sunbathing with sunglasses
- child pushing a grown-up in a stroller
- mail carrier pushing a house vacuum cleaner
- plane flying upside down in the sky
- balloon sign is written upside down

Page 31—School Scene
- teacher wearing pajamas
- desk only has three legs
- computer sitting in a small pool
- wastebasket is on the ceiling
- clock does not have any hands
- table has elephant legs

Page 32—Park Scene
- tree growing upside down
- woman pushing a wheelbarrow with a baby in it
- fish is in a bird's nest
- park sign is upside down
- flowers are small umbrellas
- children wearing ice skates on grass

Find the Mistakes

Find the Mistakes

Find the Mistakes

30

Find the Mistakes

Find the Mistakes

32

Following Directions

Procedure

1. Ask the children to sit in a circle, listen to the directions, and then follow them.

2. Read each child one of the directions below. Make substitutions as needed to accommodate a particular classroom setting or the items in the classroom.

Directions

1. Stand *near* the window.

2. Walk *around* the table.

3. Reach *up* high.

4. Walk *toward* the computer.

5. Crawl *between* _____ and _____.
   (classmate's name)   (classmate's name)

6. Skip *through* the doorway.

7. Stand *below* the clock.

8. Skip *around* the table.

9. Climb *on top of* the table.

10. Hop on two feet *in front of* the windows.

11. Hop on one foot *beside* the table.

12. Sit *in front of* the bookcase.

13. Hop *over* the book.

14. Tiptoe *behind* _____.
    (classmate's name)

15. Crawl *under* the table.

16. Climb *in* the box.

17. Hop on two feet *beside* the chalkboard.

18. Sit *by* the toy shelf.

19. Sit *next to* the easel.

20. Touch *the bottom of* the bulletin board.

Match the Shape

Materials

- Shape Cards (this page and pages 35–44)
- construction paper
- markers
- dry-erase marker

Directions for the Teacher

1. Make copies of the Shape Cards on this page and on pages 35–44.
2. Color, cut out, and mount the cards onto construction paper. Laminate the cards.

Procedure

1. Present one card to each child. Ask him or her to look at the first shape on the left. Find the matching shape on the right.

2. After introducing this activity to the class, use it again for independent learning during free play. Provide a child with a dry-erase marker and let him or her circle the correct answer on each laminated card.

3. After reviewing the child's work, clean the cards with a paper towel so another child can have a turn with this matching activity.

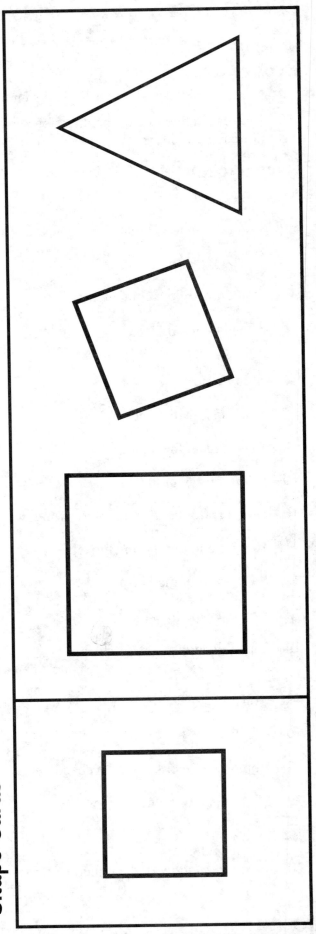

Shape Cards

Shape Cards (cont.)

Shape Cards (cont.)

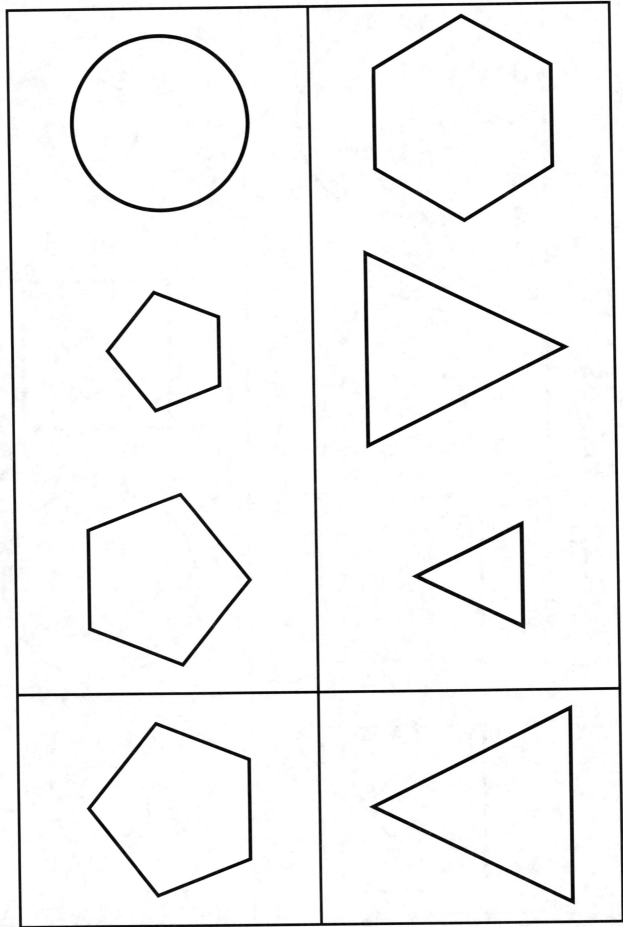

Shape Cards (cont.)

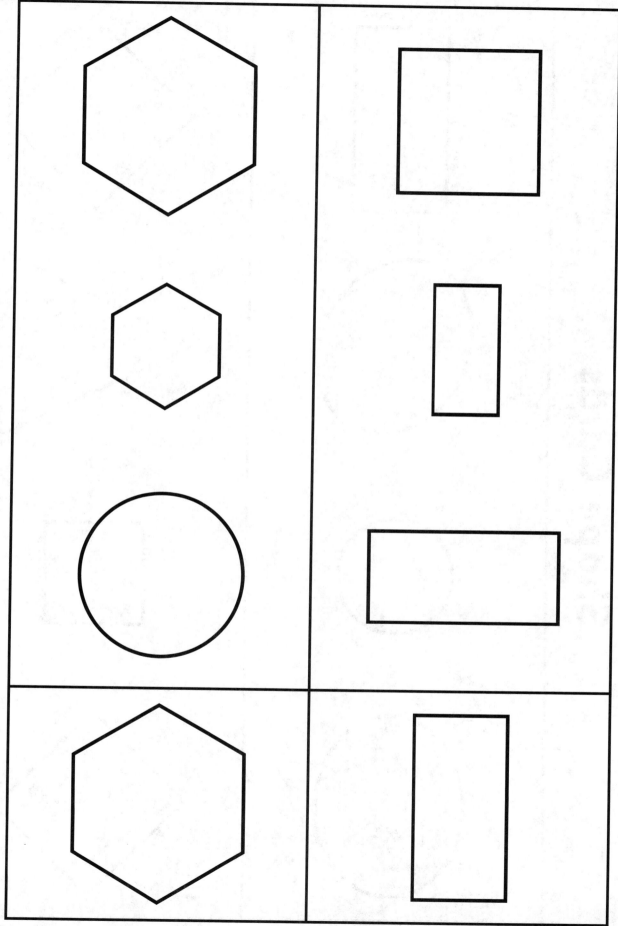

Shape Cards (cont.)

Shape Cards (cont.)

Shape Cards *(cont.)*

Shape Cards (cont.)

Shape Cards *(cont.)*

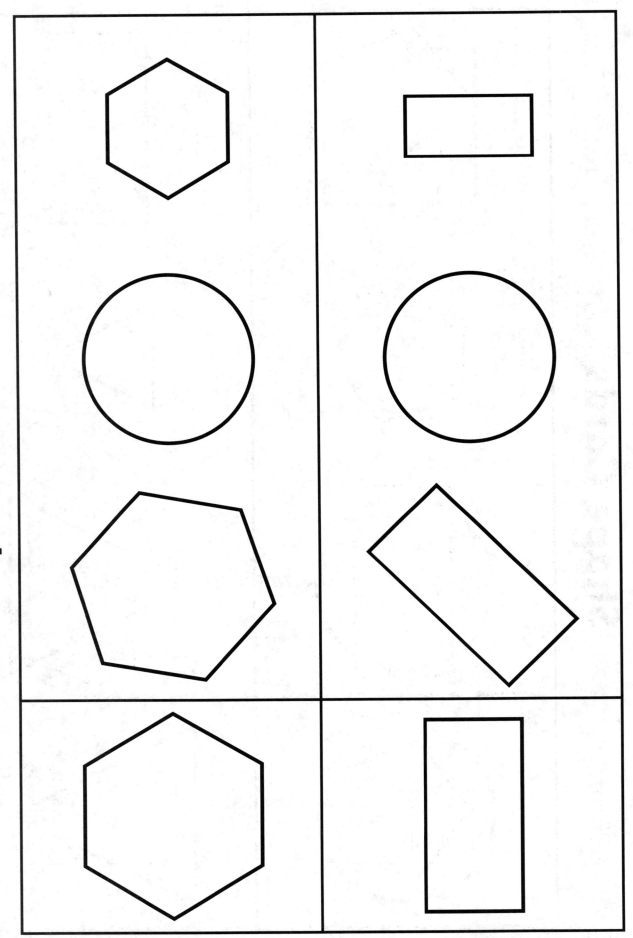

Shape Cards *(cont.)*

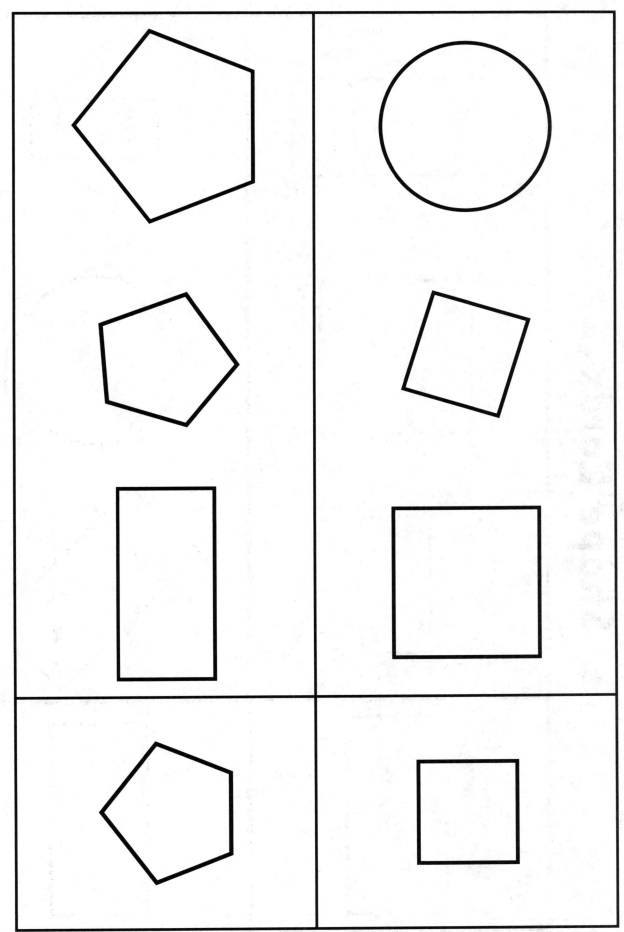

Shape Cards *(cont.)*

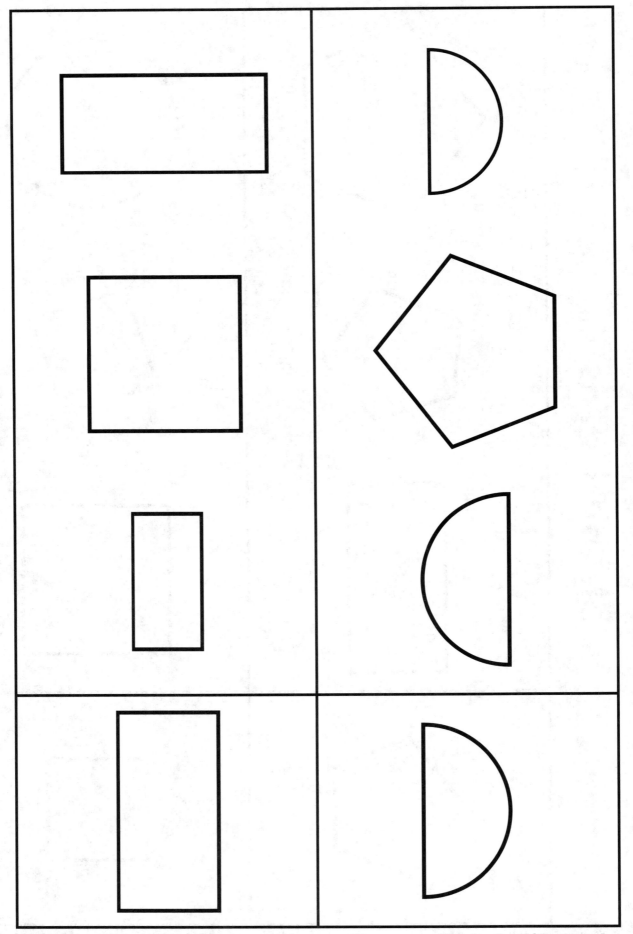

Memory Masters

Materials

- assortment of objects that complement a unit of study (e.g., classroom tools, flat or solid shapes, letters of the alphabet)
- bag or towel
- flat tray

Directions for the Teacher

1. Display the items on a flat tray so all the children can clearly see them.

Procedure

1. Ask the children to carefully study the tray of items.
2. Next, instruct the class to close their eyes and/or put their heads down.
3. Quietly remove and hide one item in a bag, or under a towel.
4. Ask the children to look up and try to decide what is missing.

Extension

Make this game more challenging by removing more than one item at a time.

Name Two Things

Procedure

1. Explain that each child will name two things that fit the description read by the teacher.

2. Give the class an example and demonstrate how to answer the question. "Name two things people use to cut. I use a *knife* and *scissors* to cut. I use a *saw* and an *ax* to cut. Both answers are correct."

3. Explain that there are many correct answers.

4. Encourage the children to answer using complete sentences.

Name Two Things Suggestions

Name two . . .

1. things people use to wash their hands.

2. animals you will see at the zoo.

3. animals found in the jungle.

4. vehicles people use for transportation.

5. places people put their money.

6. red foods.

7. Thanksgiving things.

8. objects that you use to take a bath.

9. kinds of sandwiches.

10. animals that are taller than an adult.

11. foods you can eat that you do not cook.

12. things that fly.

13. clothing items that come in pairs.

14. items found in the kitchen that can break.

15. items in your bedroom.

16. objects in the library.

17. foods you like to eat.

18. parts of a book.

19. places you like to visit.

20. kinds of toys.

Opposite Relationships

Procedure

1. Tell the children that you will read a sentence about two opposite things. Their job is to tell you which word(s) is missing.

2. Read one sentence to each child. Each sentence will have a clue about the opposite word. Give an example such as:
   If I throw a ball up, then it will (fall down.)

Opposite Sentences

1. If soup is hot, then ice cream is _____ . **COLD**

2. If a rock is hard, then cotton is _____ . **SOFT**

3. If a daddy is tall, then a child is _____ . **SHORT**

4. If the sun is out in the day, the moon is out in the _____ . **NIGHT**

5. If snow is white, then a very dark cat is _____ . **BLACK**

6. If a boy is a brother, a girl is a _____ . **SISTER**

7. If a red light means stop, then a green light means _____ . **GO**

8. If a turtle walks slow, then a lizard walks _____ . **FAST**

9. If a rocket goes up, then a parachute comes _____ . **DOWN**

10. If the ceiling is high, then the floor is _____ . **LOW**

11. If a rock is heavy, then a feather is _____ . **LIGHT**

12. If a train goes quickly, then a turtle goes _____ . **SLOWLY**

13. If laughing means happy, then crying means _____ . **SAD**

14. If a father is a man, then a mother is a _____ . **WOMAN**

15. If a whale is big, then a rabbit is _____ . **SMALL**

16. If you take a bath when you are dirty, afterwards you are _____ . **CLEAN**

17. If white is a light color, then black is a _____ . **DARK COLOR**

18. If a baby is young, then a grandma is _____ . **OLD**

19. If this is my left hand, then this must be my _____ . **RIGHT HAND**

20. If I say hello when I first see you, when I leave I will say _____ . **GOOD–BYE**

Personal Safety

Materials

- Personal Safety Certificate (page 49)
- copy of each child's personal information (You may use the form on page 49.)

Directions for the Teacher

1. Make a copy of the Personal Safety Certificate on page 49 for each child.

2. Make a copy of each child's personal information.

   - child's full name

   - parents' (guardians') full names

   - address with zip code

   - phone numbers with area codes

Personal Identification Card		
Child's Full Name		
Tammy	Sue	Brown
Parents' (Guardians) Names		
Bobbie Brown		Billy Brown
Address with Zip Code	**Phone Numbers with Area Codes**	
889 Robin St.	(999) 555-8888	
Green River, MN		
00900		

3. Present each child with a certificate as a reward for learning his or her personal information.

Procedure

Use different activities throughout the school year to help children remember personal information that will help keep them safe. The list below provides 15 suggestions to implement during the year.

1. Ask each child to say his or her full name.

2. Take roll, calling out only last names.

3. Ask each child his or her parents' names.

4. Ask, "Who has parents with the first names _____ and _____?" (Example: Betty and Bill)

5. Ask, "Who lives at _____?" (Give a number and street name.)

6. Ask each child to tell the name of his or her street.

7. Ask each child to state the number on his or her house, apartment, etc.

8. Ask each student to recite his or her city of residence.

9. Ask each child to name his or her state of residence.

10. Ask each child to recite his or her full address.

11. Ask, "Whose phone number is . . . ?" (Give a phone number with an area code.)

12. Ask each child to recite his or her phone number.

13. Ask each child to recite his or her phone area code.

14. Ask each child to recite his or her zip code.

15. Ask each child to recite the general emergency number (9-1-1).

Personal Safety Certificate

This certificate is awarded to

_____

name of student

for reciting his or her:

- first and last name
- parents' first and last names
- complete address
- phone number with area code
- emergency phone number (9-1-1)

Signed by:

_____

Classroom Teacher

_____

Date

Personal Identification Card

Child's Full Name

_____

Parents' (Guardians') Names

_____

Address with Zip Code

_____

_____

Phone Numbers with Area Codes

_____

_____

Predicting

Materials

- Prediction Chart (page 51)
- small manipulatives (e.g., cotton balls, cube blocks, stringing beads)
- small scoop (¼-cup measuring cup or laundry scoop)
- small bowl
- dry-erase marker
- construction paper

Prediction Chart		
The action: _____		
What we think will happen: _____		
Child's name	Prediction	Actual Amount

Directions for the Teacher

1. Copy the Prediction Chart on page 51.
2. Mount the chart onto construction paper and laminate it for durability.
3. Place the manipulatives in a small bowl.
4. Use a dry-erase marker to fill in the chart.

Procedure

1. Ask each child to predict how many items he or she will be able to pick up in one scoop.
2. Write each child's prediction on the Prediction Chart.
3. Let each child have a turn using the scoop.
4. Count the actual number of items in the scoop and record the information on the Prediction Chart.

Prediction Chart

The action:_____.

What we think will happen:_____

_____.

Child's Name	Prediction	Actual Amount

Recognizing Similarities and Differences

Materials

- 2 hula hoops or rope

Directions for the Teacher

1. Lay down two hula hoops, or use pieces of rope to create two circles on the floor.

Procedure

1. Select two children at a time to stand in the hoops.

2. Ask the students to identify one thing that is the same about the two children. Review the definition of "the same." (Examples: They are the same because they both have on shorts. They are the same because they both have on white socks.)

3. Next, ask the students to identify one thing that is different about the two children. Review the definition of "different." (Examples: They are different because one has glasses and the other does not. They are different because one is a boy and one is a girl.)

4. Allow each child to have a turn standing in a hula hoop.

5. Encourage the children to speak in complete sentences and use their classmates' names.

Extension

1. Select one child to stand in front of the class. Ask the class to take a good look at this classmate.

2. Have the children close and cover their eyes.

3. Change one thing about the selected child. (Examples: Roll up a sleeve, remove a shoe, turn the child backward.)

4. Ask the children to uncover their eyes and raise their hands if they can identify what is **different** about their classmate.

Rhyming Riddles—Animals

Materials

- Animal Cards (pages 55–59)
- Animal Rhymes (below and page 54)
- construction paper
- markers

Directions for the Teacher

1. Make copies of the Animal Rhymes below and on page 54 and the Animal Cards on pages 55–59.
2. Color, cut out, and mount the cards onto construction paper. Laminate the cards.

Procedure

1. Display the Animal Cards so all the children can see them.
2. Read one rhyme card to each child, leaving off the animal's name at the end. Let him or her choose the appropriate picture card that corresponds with the rhyme.
3. Older children can do this activity without the aid of the Animal Cards.

Animal Rhymes

I am green, I croak a lot, And I leap from spot to spot. I can sit upon a log. I like water, I am a **FROG**.	Animals know that I am king. I can scare most anything. Call me Leo, call me Brian, Either way I am a **LION**.
I can swing from tree to tree, And bananas are for me. I am funny, and I am spunky. A long tail proves I am a **MONKEY**.	I like honey, yes I do, And I sleep all winter, too. A fur coat is what I wear. Now you know, I am a **BEAR**.
I have wool, and I can bleat. I like clover leaves to eat. My little baby likes to leap. He is a lamb. I am a **SHEEP**.	My fur is black and white. And, I like to hunt at night. I have stripes like a chipmunk. I am stinky. I'm a **SKUNK**.

Animal Rhymes *(cont.)*

I hang upside down when I sleep. Shh, please do not make a peep. I am not a cat or rat. Surely, you know that I am a **BAT.**	I might live in rocks or trees. I do not have legs or knees. In answering, there is no mistake. I have scaly skin. I am a **SNAKE.**
I am an animal of medium size. I have a mask around my eyes. I hunt for food under the moon. You might see me, I am a **RACCOON.**	I live in the ocean blue. I am a huge animal, too. No way can I fit in a pail! You have guessed, I am a **WHALE.**
I like milk, yes I do. I chase mice, how about you? I like to sleep, what about that? You must know that I am a **CAT.**	My nest is a place I like to be, To keep my babies safe with me. I like to fly, I am sure you have heard. My feathers tell you I am a **BIRD.**
I am man's best friend, you see. Bones are a special treat for me. I can run with you as you jog. You can tell that I am a **DOG.**	I am the same shape as a horse. But I am different—of course. My stripes make people "ooh" and "aah," And tell you I am a **ZEBRA.**
I am enormous, and I am gray. With my trunk, I pick up hay. I am never called a runt, For I am an **ELEPHANT.**	The zoo is where you will find me. My fur has a pattern, you see. My long neck will make you laugh. You have guessed, I am a **GIRAFFE.**
I just like to eat and grunt. If I am small, I am called a runt. With my snout, I root and dig. I am so noisy. I am a **PIG.**	My home is in the deep blue sea. People can be afraid of me. I like to swim around in the dark. As you have guessed, I am a **SHARK**
I have a beard and knobby horns. I live in a barn, and I eat corn. Careful, or I will eat your coat, Because I am a hungry **GOAT.**	My home is on a peaceful farm. I will not cause you any harm. I'll give you milk if you ask me how. I am your friend, a great big **COW.**

Animal Cards

Animal Cards *(cont.)*

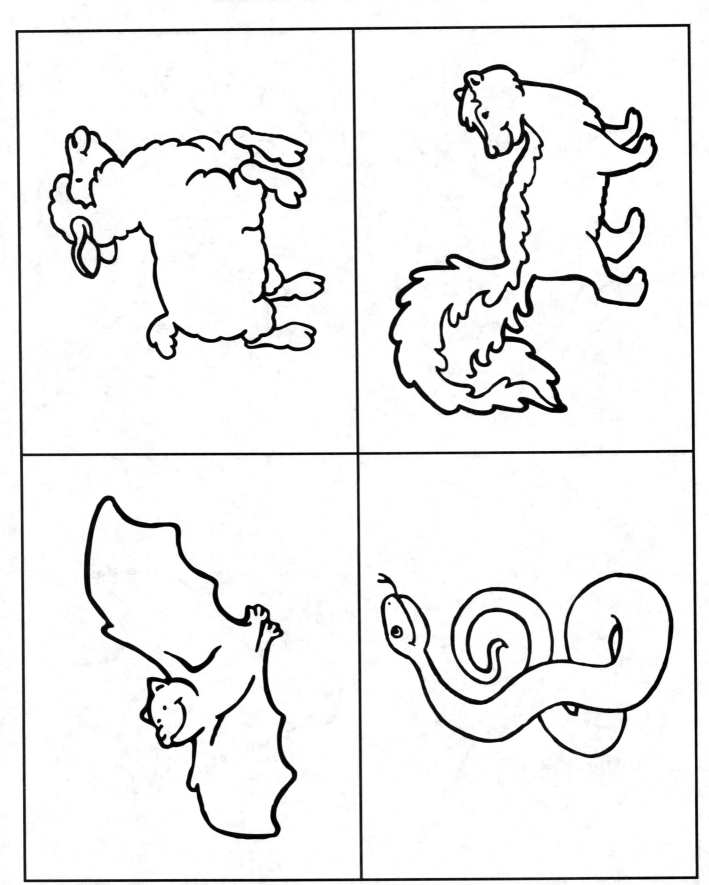

Animal Cards *(cont.)*

Animal Cards *(cont.)*

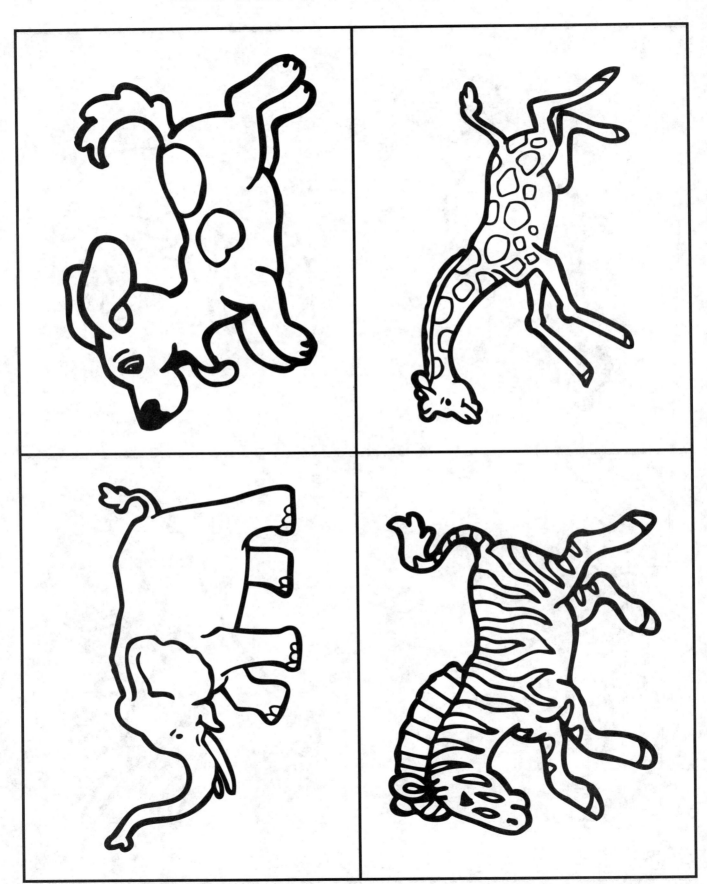

Animal Cards *(cont.)*

Rhyming Riddles—Objects

Materials
- Object Cards (pages 61–65)
- construction paper

Directions for the Teacher
1. Copy the Object Cards on pages 61–65.
2. Color, cut out, and mount the cards onto construction paper. Laminate the cards.

Procedure
1. Display the cards so all the children can see them.
2. Read one rhyme to each child and allow him or her to choose the card that corresponds with the rhyme.
3. Older children can do this activity without the aid of the cards.

Object Rhymes

1. Apples grow on a _____ .
   It rhymes with **bee**. **TREE**

2. You drive in a _____ .
   It rhymes with **bar**. **CAR**

3. You bounce a _____ .
   It rhymes with **tall**. **BALL**

4. On your head, you wear a _____ .
   It rhymes with **cat**. **HAT**

5. The _____ shines at night.
   It rhymes with **spoon**. **MOON**

6. On your foot, you wear a _____ .
   It rhymes with **boo**. **SHOE**

7. You use your _____ to smell.
   It rhymes with **hose**. **NOSE**

8. You sit on a _____ .
   It rhymes with **bear**. **CHAIR**

9. You see with your _____ .
   It rhymes with **pie**. **EYE**

10. On your finger, you wear a _____ .
    It rhymes with **sing**. **RING**

11. You read a _____ .
    It rhymes with **hook**. **BOOK**

12. A _____ gives light.
    It rhymes with **camp**. **LAMP**

13. You may live in a _____ .
    It rhymes with **mouse**. **HOUSE**

14. You fly in a _____ .
    It rhymes with **crane**. **PLANE**

15. On a cold day, you wear a _____ .
    It rhymes with **boat**. **COAT**

16. _____ is a sweet treat.
    It rhymes with **dandy**. **CANDY**

17. In the sky, you can see the _____ .
    It rhymes with **fun**. **SUN**

18. Please open the _____ .
    It rhymes with **floor**. **DOOR**

19. You sleep on a _____ .
    It rhymes with **red**. **BED**

20. You eat soup with a _____ .
    It rhymes with **moon**. **SPOON**

Object Cards

Object Cards *(cont.)*

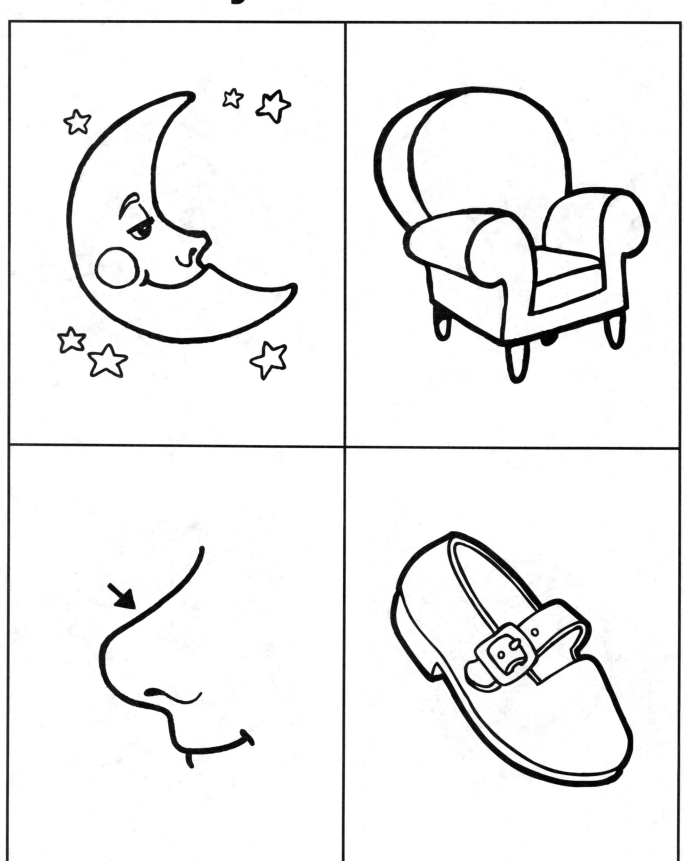

Object Cards *(cont.)*

Object Cards *(cont.)*

Object Cards *(cont.)*

Rhyming Pairs

Materials

- Rhyming Pair Cards (pages 67–72)
- construction paper

Directions for the Teacher

1. Copy the Rhyming Pair Cards on pages 67–72.
2. Color, cut out, and mount the cards onto construction paper. Laminate the cards.

Procedure

1. Use the Rhyming Pair Cards for the following three activities:

Find the Rhyming Pair

1. Set out one-half of each rhyming pair, so the cards are easy for the children to see. (A short portable easel will help display the cards for better viewing.) Initially, it may be helpful to set 4–5 cards on the easel so the child does not have to look through many cards to find his or her match.
2. Distribute the matching rhyme cards to the students.
3. Let each child have a turn finding a card that will rhyme with the one in his or her hand.
4. Encourage the child to say the rhyming words and return the cards to the teacher.

Stand Up for Rhymes!

1. Distribute all the cards to the children in the group. Make sure all the matching pairs are used. Have one child stand up and say his or her rhyming word. The child that has the matching card will acknowledge that he or she has the matching card by also standing.
2. Together, they will return their cards to the teacher and say the rhyming words.

Rhyming Memory Game

1. Mix up some of the pairs of cards. Place them face down on the floor.
2. The teacher turns over two cards and says the two words to identify the cards.
3. The children respond by saying, "rhymes" or "does not rhyme."
4. Then let each child have a turn selecting two cards to find a match.

Rhymes

Does Not Rhyme

Rhyming Pair Cards

Rhyming Pair Cards *(cont.)*

Rhyming Pair Cards *(cont.)*

Rhyming Pair Cards *(cont.)*

Rhyming Pair Cards *(cont.)*

Rhyming Pair Cards *(cont.)*

Spatial Concepts

Materials

- small action figure or toy
- construction paper
- shape patterns

Directions for the Teacher

1. Choose a small action figure or toy.
2. Prepare four construction-paper shapes: circle, square, triangle and rectangle. Each shape should be large enough to cover the action figure or toy.
3. Make appropriate substitutions to complement teaching objectives.

Procedure

1. For this activity a circle, square, triangle, and rectangle are used. Place the shapes in this order in front of the children. Leave a small space between the shapes. The circle should be on the left when viewed by the children.
2. Read one direction to each child. Have the child do the action.

Directions

Place the toy . . .

1. *under* the square.
2. *next* to the triangle.
3. *between* the triangle and rectangle.
4. *in front of* the circle.
5. *far away from* the rectangle.
6. *on the left side of* the square.
7. *near* the circle, but not on it.
8. *at the bottom of* the triangle.
9. *on the middle of* the square.
10. *on the right side of* the rectangle.
11. *close to* the circle.
12. *between* the circle and you.
13. *next to* the square.
14. *on top of* the triangle.
15. *in back of* the rectangle.
16. *over* the circle.
17. *below* the triangle.
18. *upside down* on the rectangle.
19. *between* the square and the triangle.
20. *in* my hand.

Tools of the Trade

Materials

- mystery bag (or box or basket)
- common tools found in the classroom (See list below for suggestions.)

Procedure

1. Place the tools in the container. Have each child select one tool and describe how it is used to the rest of the class.

2. Encourage the children to speak using complete sentences.

3. Provide more tools than children, so each child will have several choices.

chalk	glue stick	paintbrush	ruler
clock	headphones	paper towel	safety scissors
clothespin	hole punch	pencil (unsharpened)	sponge
crayon	lunch box	pencil sharpener	stamp pad
eraser	marker	pointer	stapler

Using a Floor Number Line

Materials

- colored tape
- ruler
- numbers in large font

0 1 2 3 4 5 6 7 8 9 10

Directions for the Teacher

1. Make a number line on the floor using colored tape. Attach the numbers 0–10 at one-foot intervals. You may wish to begin with 0–5 and add numbers as students' skills improve. (See diagram below.)

Procedure

1. Use the directions below to teach the following number concepts:

   A. Recognizing numbers—Stand on _____.
   (say a number)

   B. Counting forward from 1 to 10—Start on zero. Jump and count forward from 1 to 10.

   C. Counting forward from a given number to 10—Start on any number. Jump and count forward until reaching 10.

   D. Counting backward from 10 to 0—Start on the number 10. Jump and count backward until reaching zero.

   E. One-to-one correspondence—Stand on any number. Jump _____ times.
   (say a number)

   F. Finding a number that comes before or after another number—Stand on the number that comes before/after _____.
   (say a number)

   G. Finding a number that falls between two other numbers—Stand on the number that comes between the numbers _____ and _____.
   (say a number)   *(say the number that is 2 more than the first number)*

   H. Adding numbers with sums up to five—Stand on _____ and add _____
   (say a number)   *(say a number)*

   by jumping that many spaces forward. Ask what the answer will be when the child is finished jumping.

   I. Subtracting numbers under ten—Stand on _____ and subtract _____
   (say a number)   *(say a number)*

by jumping that many spaces backward. Ask what the answer will be when the child is finished jumping.

What Am I?

Materials

- All Around Me Cards (pages 77–81)
- markers
- construction paper

Directions for the Teacher

1. Copy the All Around Me Cards on pages 77–81.
2. Color, cut out, and mount the cards onto construction paper. Laminate the cards.

Procedure

1. Display 6–10 cards at a time for the children to see.
2. Read an appropriate set of clues to each child and let him or her select the corresponding card.
3. As each child selects one card, add another card to the collection. This ensures that each child will have the same number of cards to look at to make a selection.
4. Eventually children will do this activity without the aid of the All Around Me Cards.

Clues for All Around Me Cards

1. I am a black and white animal. I live at the South Pole. I eat fish and like to swim. **PENGUIN**

2. I am something you wear. I may have buttons. I am worn at nighttime, and I have a top and bottom. **PAJAMAS**

3. I am used to travel. I float on water. I may have a horn and a captain. **BOAT/SHIP**

4. I am an animal. I move slowly. I carry my home with me, and I have a shell. **TURTLE**

5. I am a special man. I make decisions. I sit on a throne, and I wear a crown. **KING**

6. I am a tool. I have teeth. I am very sharp, and I cut wood. **SAW**

7. I am a kind of furniture. I am usually in the living room. I may have pillows, and I am used for sitting. **COUCH / SOFA**

8. I am something that grows. I attract bees. I smell good, and I make beautiful bouquets. **FLOWER**

9. I help people. I wear a special uniform. I use a hose, and I put out fires. **FIREFIGHTER**

10. I am an animal. I have a long tail. I have big ears, and I eat cheese. **MOUSE**

11. I am a food. I grow in a field. I have a husk, and I am yellow. **CORN**

12. I am a toy. I am fun to ride. I have two wheels, and I may have a bell. **BIKE**

13. I am an animal. I am from Australia. My legs help me hop, and my baby rides in my pouch. **KANGAROO**

14. I am a fruit. I grow in the summer. I am green and red, and I can have many seeds. **WATERMELON**

15. I am used to travel a long distance. I can be very long. I go very fast, and I have a caboose. **TRAIN**

16. I am a person. I work at a school. I help you learn the ABC's, and I am your friend. **TEACHER**

17. I am funny. I wear colorful clothes. I have a silly nose, and I work at the circus. **CLOWN**

18. I am a food. I grow on a tree. I can be red, yellow, or green. Worms like me! **APPLE**

19. I am used for art. I have many colors. Put me on paper with a brush to make a picture. **PAINT**

20. I show the date. I list the days of the week. I have numbers, and I tell the year. **CALENDAR**

All Around Me Cards

All Around Me Cards *(cont.)*

All Around Me Cards *(cont.)*

All Around Me Cards (cont.)

All Around Me Cards *(cont.)*

What Am I?

Materials
- Body Part Cards (pages 83–87)
- markers
- construction paper

Directions for the Teacher
1. Make copies of the Body Part Cards on pages 83–87.
2. Color, cut out, and mount the cards onto construction paper. Laminate the cards.

Procedure
1. Explain to the children that for this activity they will be identifying body parts after listening to important clues.
2. Set the cards out so all the children can see them.
3. Read one group of clues at a time. Use the phrase, "What am I?" after each.
4. Complete this activity with the whole group or with one child at a time.
5. For young children, only use a few cards at a time. For older children, do not use the Body Part Cards to make this an auditory game.

Clues for Body Part Cards

1. I like to wiggle in my socks, and I have ten parts. **TOES**
2. I am attached to your eyelids. I protect your eyes from dust and dirt. **EYELASHES**
3. I help your leg bend. Put a bandage on me when I have an accident. **KNEE**
4. I hold your watch; please do not make it too tight! **WRIST**
5. I like to scratch, and I have four on each hand and a thumb. **FINGERS**
6. I growl when you are hungry, and you feed me food. **STOMACH**
7. I hold up your head, and you keep me warm with a scarf. **NECK**
8. I attach your foot and leg, and I do not like sprains. **ANKLE**
9. I am used for walking, and I do not like hot cement. **FEET**

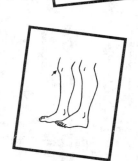

10. I help you breathe, and you use a tissue to keep me clear. **NOSE**
11. I cover your head, and I come in different colors and lengths. **HAIR**
12. I am used to listen to sounds, but I do not like loud noises. **EARS**
13. I help bend your arm, and I am in the middle of it. **ELBOW**
14. I protect your spine, and I go from your head to your bottom. **BACK**
15. I help you speak, and I help you eat and sing. **MOUTH**
16. I am in the middle of your stomach, and I am an "innie" or "outie." **BELLY BUTTON**
17. I am on your face, and I turn red when I get embarrassed. **CHEEKS**
18. I hang from your shoulders, and I can give a good hug. **ARMS**
19. I am hard and white. I break up food to help you eat. I can fall out. **TEETH**
20. You can shrug me. Your arms are attached to me. **SHOULDERS**

Body Part Cards

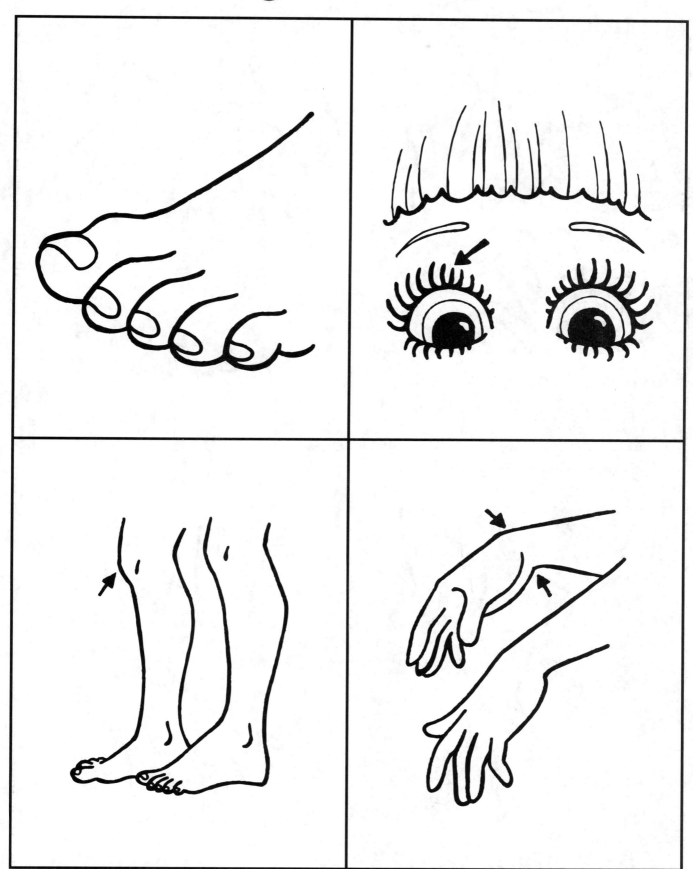

Body Part Cards *(cont.)*

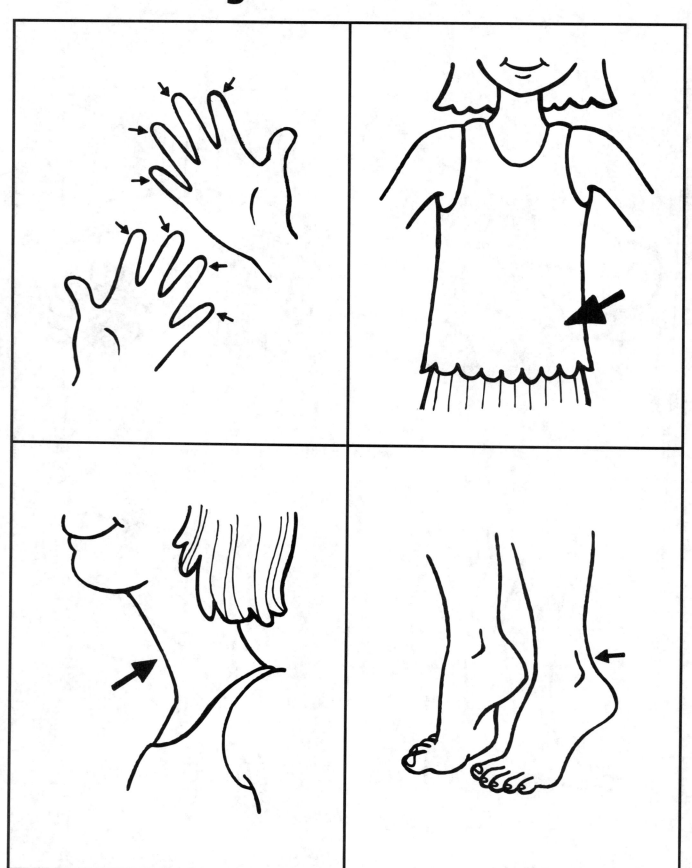

Body Part Cards *(cont.)*

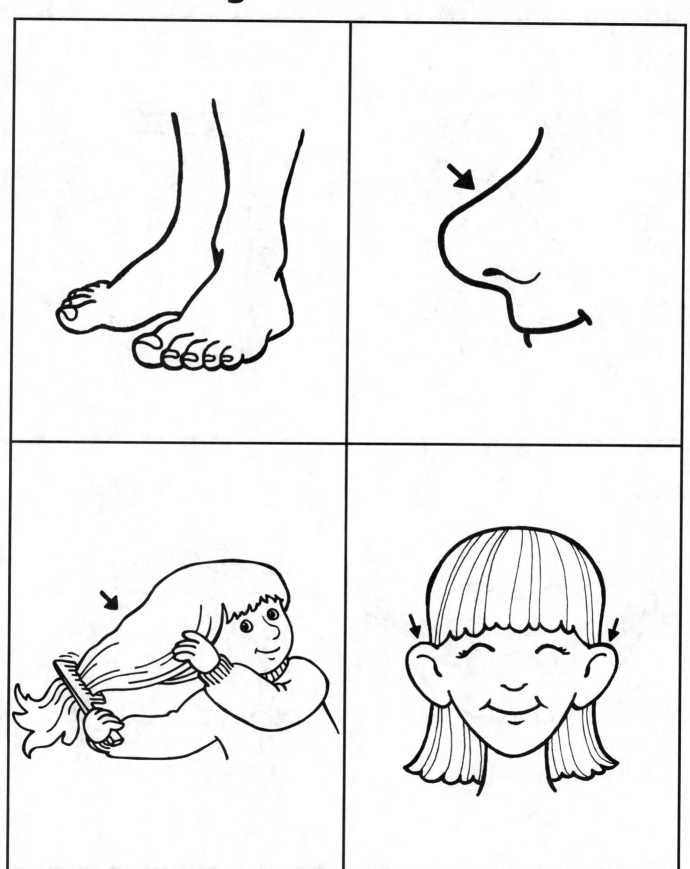

Body Part Cards *(cont.)*

Body Part Cards *(cont.)*

What Does Not Belong?

Materials

- What Does Not Belong? Cards (this page and pages 89–98)
- markers
- construction paper

Directions for the Teacher

1. Copy the What Does Not Belong? Cards on this page and pages 89–98.
2. Color, cut out, and mount the cards onto construction paper. Laminate the cards.

Procedure

1. Show one card to each child and ask him or her to tell which item does not belong.
2. Ask the child to explain why it does not belong.
3. Encourage the children to speak using complete sentences.

What Does Not Belong? Cards

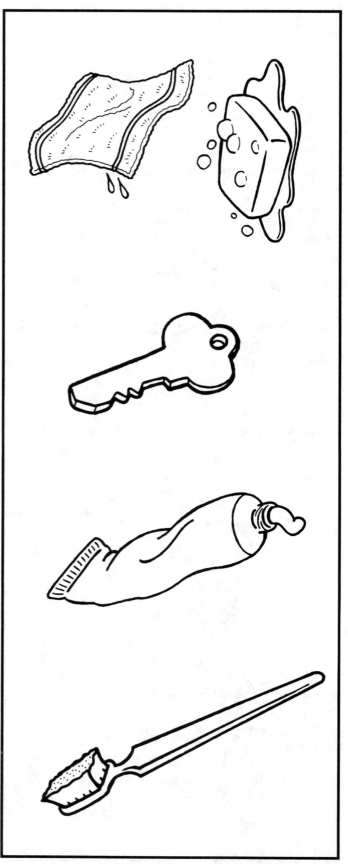

What Does Not Belong? Cards *(cont.)*

What Does Not Belong? Cards *(cont.)*

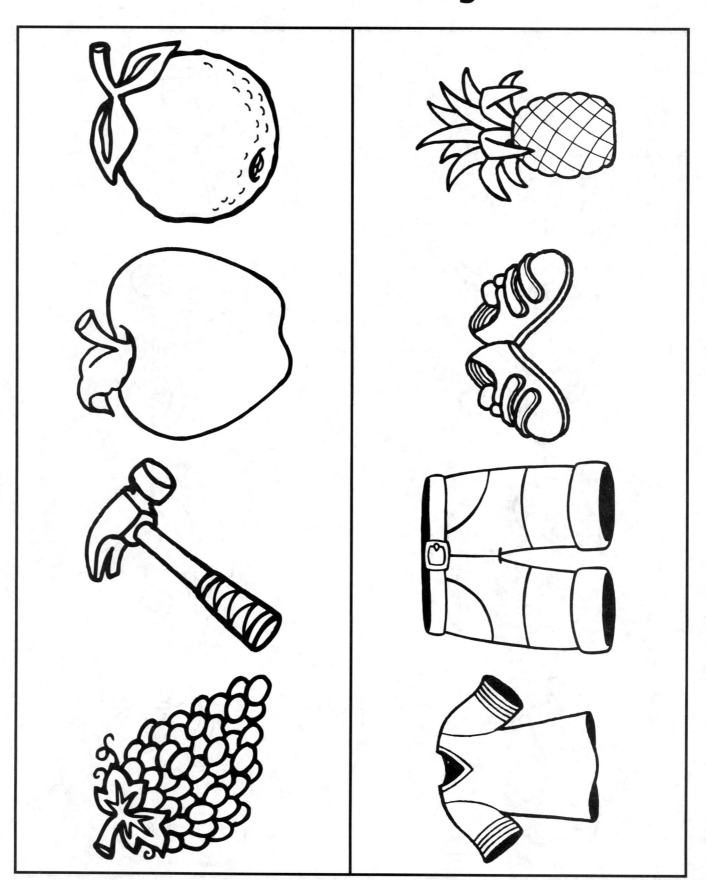

What Does Not Belong? Cards *(cont.)*

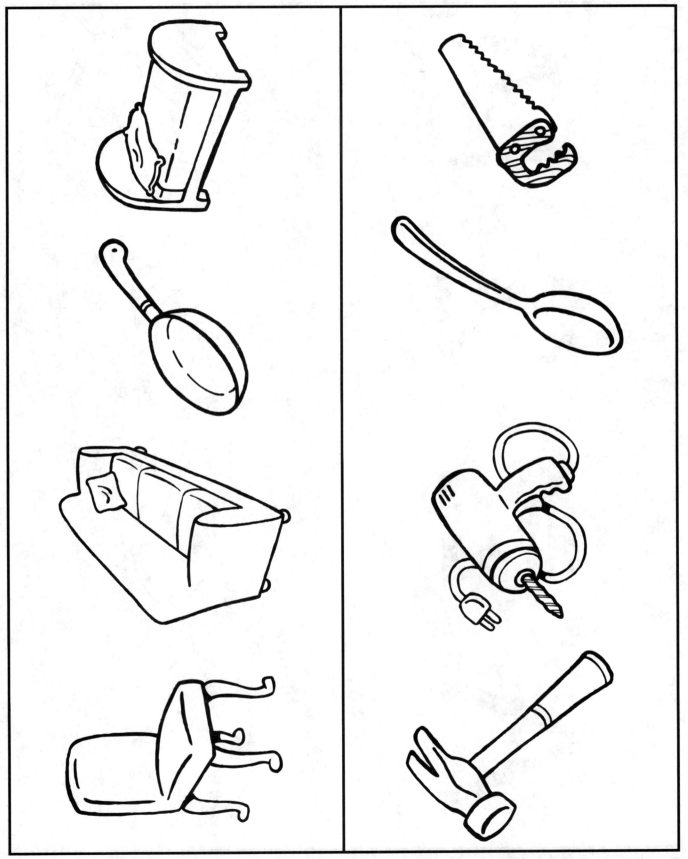

What Does Not Belong? Cards (cont.)

What Does Not Belong? Cards *(cont.)*

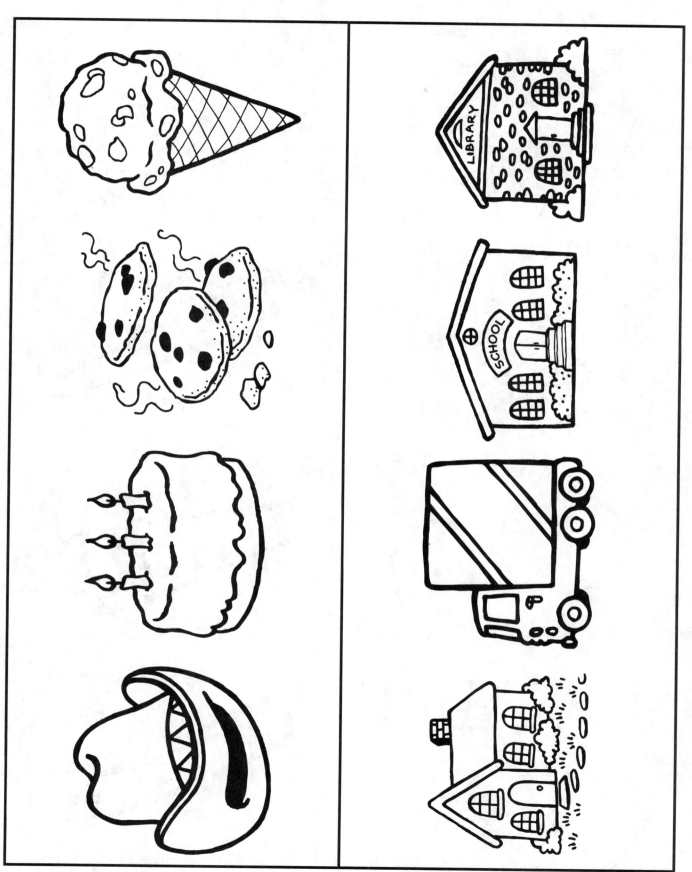

What Does Not Belong? Cards *(cont.)*

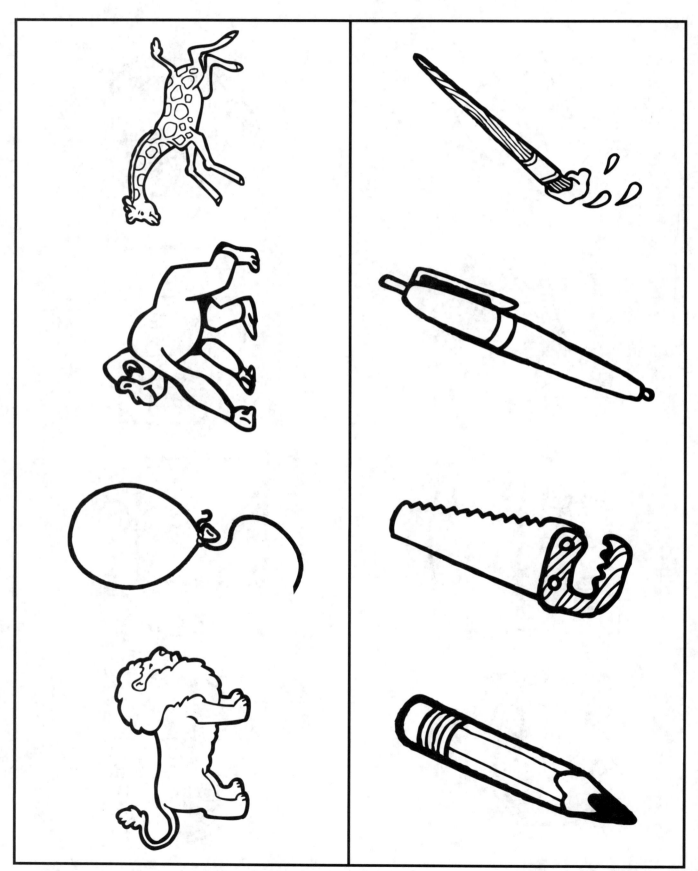

What Does Not Belong? Cards *(cont.)*

What Does Not Belong? Cards *(cont.)*

What Does Not Belong? Cards *(cont.)*

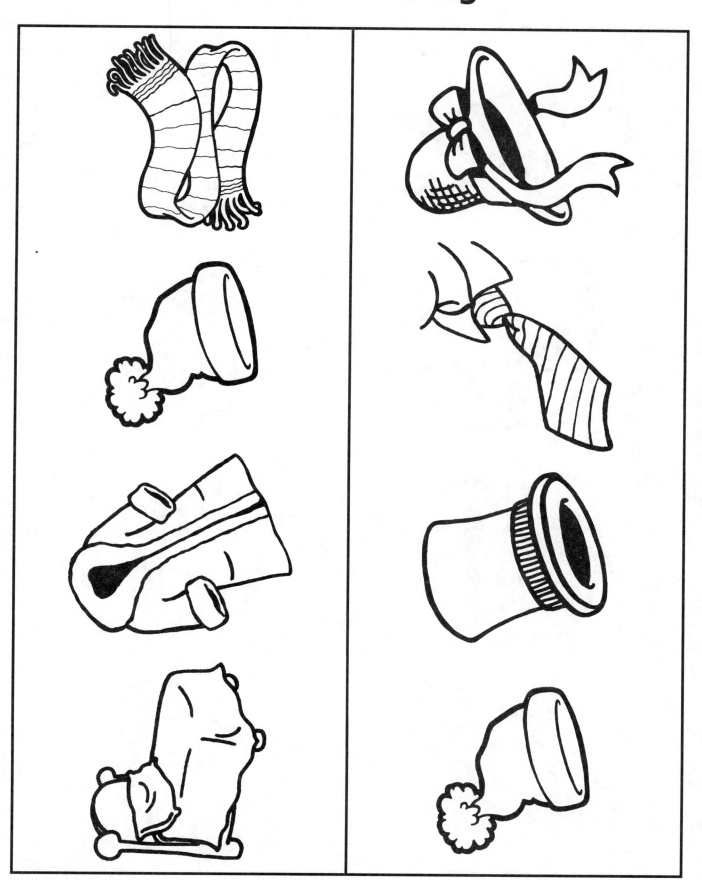

What Does Not Belong? Cards (cont.)

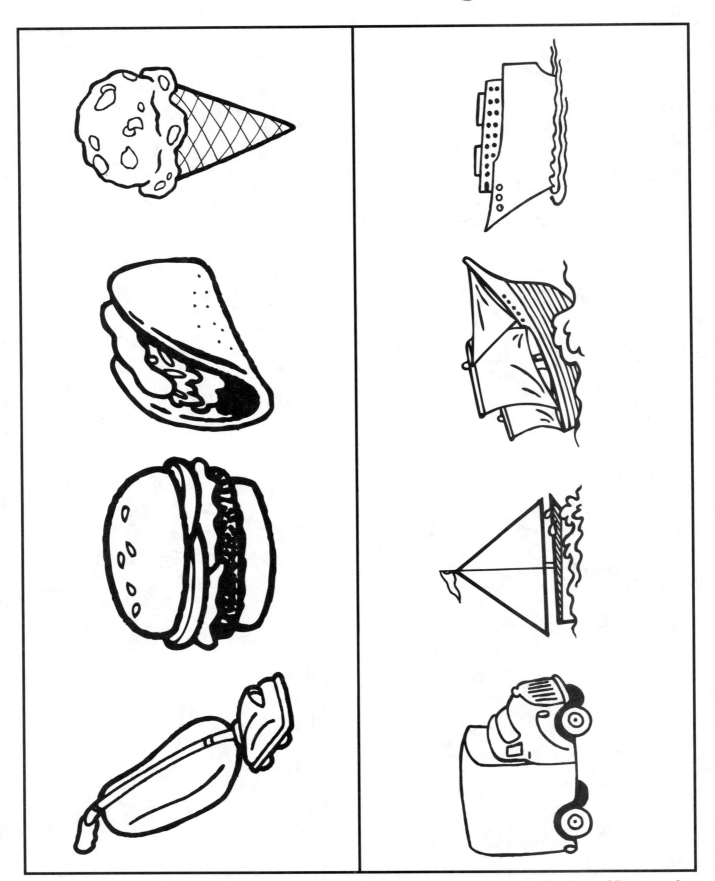

What Goes Together?

Materials

- What Goes Together? Cards (below and pages 100–105)
- markers
- construction paper

Directions for the Teacher

1. Copy the cards below and on pages 100–105.
2. Color, cut out, and mount the cards onto construction paper. Laminate the cards.

Procedure

1. Scatter several matching sets of cards in front of the children.

2. One at a time, ask a child to find two cards that go together.

3. Have each child explain why the two objects go together.

4. Add new cards after each child removes a set. This ensures that every child can choose from several cards. **Hint:** Do not place matching cards next to each other when displaying them.

What Goes Together? Cards *(cont.)*

What Goes Together? Cards *(cont.)*

What Goes Together? Cards *(cont.)*

What Goes Together? Cards *(cont.)*

What Goes Together? Cards *(cont.)*

What Goes Together? Cards *(cont.)*

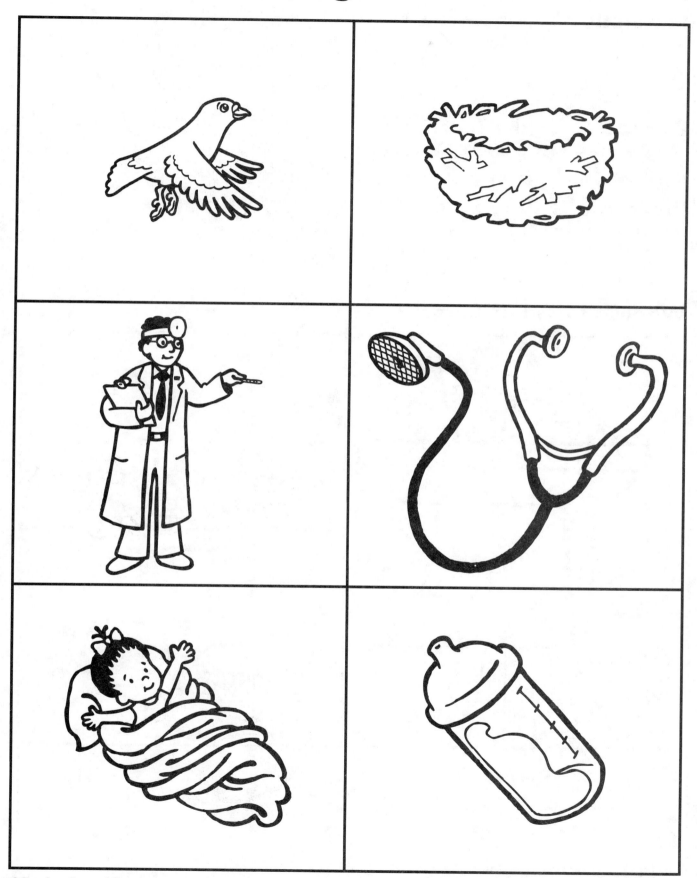

What Is Missing?

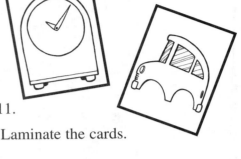

Materials

- What Is Missing? Cards (below and on pages 107–111)
- markers
- construction paper

Directions for the Teacher

1. Copy the What Is Missing? Cards below and on pages 107-111.
2. Color, cut out, and mount the cards onto construction paper. Laminate the cards.

Procedure

1. Give each child a different card. Ask, "What is missing?"
2. Ask children to tell you how the missing part would affect the object.

What Is Missing? Cards

What Is Missing? Cards *(cont.)*

What Is Missing? Cards *(cont.)*